No More Victims

Protecting Those with Autism from Cyber Bullying, Internet Predators & Scams

Dr Jed Baker, author of *No More Meltdowns*

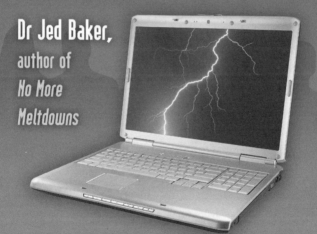

Additional material provided by Jennifer McIlwee Myers

No More Victims:
Protecting Those with Autism from Cyber Bullying, Internet Predators & Scams

All marketing and publishing rights guaranteed to and reserved by:

FUTURE HORIZONS INC.

721 W. Abram Street

Arlington, TX 76013

(800) 489-0727

(817) 277-0727

(817) 277-2270 (fax)

E-mail: *info@fhautism.com*

www.fhautism.com

ISBN: 978-1-935274-92-6

WITHDRAWN
From the
Mish Penn Harris Public Library

The digital world of cell phones and other Internet devices offers a wonderful way to communicate and socialize with others. Yet, it is also rife with dangers of being victimized emotionally, physically, and financially. In this book, I address three main areas of concern that pertain especially to individuals with autism spectrum disorders: cyber bullying, online sexual predators, and Internet scams.

Individuals on the autism spectrum may be particularly susceptible to these types of scams because of challenges with being able to gauge and understand others' intentions, isolation, increased time online, and difficulty with developing assertive communication skills. It can be hard for them to determine when an online perpetrator may be bullying or trying to exploit someone, if they have difficulty with perspective taking and understanding other people's motives and intent. The social isolation individuals on the spectrum experience makes them more likely to spend time online and more apt to respond to online scammers and predators who offer friendship, romance, or other rewards. Finally, difficulty with communication skills may make it especially challenging to seek help or end communications with online perpetrators.

I have based the advice in this book on current research about cyber bullying, online predators, and scams. However, there is no substitute for hearing the perspective of someone on the spectrum who negotiates the dangers of the digital world on a daily basis. Thus, Chapter 5 features Jennifer McIlwee Myers, an insightful author with Asperger's syndrome. She provides an insider's view of how she stays safe on the Internet. She also explains what parents and others can do to help their loved ones use the Internet safely.

1

Types of Internet Victimization

Cyber Bullying is a term typically used to describe emotional victimization and abuse among school- and college-aged individuals. It occurs via the Internet or through digital means. Students may use the Internet to harass, intimidate, or bully others. Cyber bullying may include:

I **Posting insulting and embarrassing information or pictures of others on a Web site**

Example: In several high schools across the country, students have been suspended or expelled after creating Web sites on which they could "rate the attractiveness" of their peers. Students who were rated as attractive, as well as those who were rated poorly, were potentially embarrassed or humiliated in a public forum.

II **Fooling victims into disclosing personal or sensitive information, which the predator(s) will later use against them**

Example: While on Facebook, one of my male students with autism spectrum disorder (ASD) received a message from a girl he knew well, saying that she really liked him and wanted to date him. She asked that he e-mail her a nude photo of himself. He sent the photo, only to find out later that he had sent the photo to someone who had posed as the girl he knew. The actual person who had requested the photo had hacked into the girl's account, posed as her to get this photo, and intended to send the picture out to students all over the school. Fortunately, the boy's parents and the police were informed. They were able to trace the source of the hacking, and they retrieved the photo before it was distributed.

III Sending threatening or insulting messages directly to victims

Example: A middle-school boy with Asperger's syndrome posted some YouTube videos of songs he wrote. Some peers from his school commented online. They demeaned the boy and his songs, calling him "retarded" and other derogatory names. The boy's parents sought help from the school and the police. The police would not get involved, and the school did not have the legal means to trace the source of the comments. In the end, the boy took down the YouTube videos and blocked comments from others.

IV **Impersonating others to send insulting or embarrassing messages**

Example: Four students who very much liked their math teacher thought it would be funny to create an Instagram account in their teacher's name. They posted his picture, which they got from Facebook, and posted information like, "I love math." What they did not bargain for was that other students, whom they had permitted to "follow" this Instagram account, posted derogatory comments about the teacher. The school traced the Instagram account to one of the student's phones and then to all four students who admitted to creating the account. The students received in-school suspensions and were asked to create a project to warn incoming middle-schoolers the following year about how to avoid cyber bullying.

Online Sexual Predators

Whereas cyber bullying is a term usually reserved for emotional abuse among peers, sexual predators use the Internet to seek out younger victims to sexually abuse. They often pose as other people to be able to befriend vulnerable children and teens. They may blackmail students into sending nude pictures of themselves and set up a meeting, where they can abuse their victims.

Internet Scams

In the adult world, cyber bullying often manifests in the form of Internet scams, where victims fall prey to those who take advantage of them—typically for financial gain. For example, on some online dating sites, predators pose as would-be dates, using fake pictures or videos to attract others and foster a trusting relationship, only to eventually try to extort money from their victims.

Who is likely to be a victim of cyber bullying, online predators, and Internet scams?

Cyber Bullying

Anyone can be victimized, not only those on the autism spectrum. For example, according to the Cyber Bullying Research Center, about 20%–25% of 11- to 18-year-olds have experienced some form of cyber bullying, and 10%–20% experience it regularly.[1] However, according to Sofronoff, Dark, and Stone, certain characteristics are associated with a greater likelihood of being bullied.[2] Passive victims tend to be physically weak, anxious, insecure, solitary, and poor at sports. Proactive victims tend to be irritating, provocative, and socially clumsy and have problems with social interaction. These two different sets of characteristics often describe individuals with ASDs, and the latter set of traits is often associated with individuals who have an ASD or attention-deficit/hyperactivity disorder (ADHD). Kowalski and Fedina examined bullying and cyber bullying among 5th to 12th graders with Asperger's syndrome and/or ADHD.[3] They found that these students were at high risk for being bullied, as compared with their typically developing peers. They also found that parents did not know how often their children had been bullied or had bullied others.

Online Predators

Wolak, Finkelhor, Mitchell, and Ybarra reviewed the research on characteristics of both online sexual predators and youth who were victimized.[4] Ninety-nine percent of young victims were between the ages of 13 and 17. Some of the risk factors associated with being a victim included a previous history of sexual abuse that may make it difficult to assess inappropriate sexual advances; interacting with strangers online, particularly in chat rooms, and engaging in conversation about sex; using rude or nasty language online; and seeking out porn. Although posting personal information about oneself is not a risk factor by itself, sharing such information directly with strangers is indeed a risk factor. It is important to note that those who are lonely, shy, depressed, and lacking in social skills may be more likely to seek out chat rooms and talk with strangers online. In this way, it is possible that socially isolated individuals with ASDs are more likely to seek out chat rooms to interact with strangers, given their lack of known friends with whom they can communicate.

Another characteristic of online predators is that the relationship fostered is conducted in secrecy, without family and friends being aware. Predators often want to turn their victims away from their families and friends, while providing their victims with the sense that only they really care for them. Once again, isolated youths with ASDs who seek the positive attention of others may be particularly vulnerable to this kind of threat.

Internet Scams

Titus and Gover reviewed some of the characteristics of those who were victims of Internet fraud and scams.[5] Contrary to popular belief, it seems that higher education does not serve as any kind of protection against this kind of threat. More highly educated people seem to have wider interests and are more involved in the marketplace and on the Internet, which increases their exposure to fraudulent solicitations. Pak and Shadel also reviewed characteristics of victims of fraud (financial investment fraud, prescription drug fraud, identity protection fraud, lottery fraud, and advanced-fee loan fraud) and identified the following traits:[6]

> ➤ Victims are less able to identify persuasion tactics and are more interested in these tactics than are the general population. The most common tactics are statements like, "You'll make a lot of money," "You can trust me," "Everyone is doing it," "Hurry—time is running out," "You're getting a really good deal," and "Do this for me—as your friend."

> ➤ Victims are more open to sales pitches.

> ➤ Victims tend to be risk takers.

> ➤ Victims tend to be unhappier than the general population.

> ➤ Victims are less concerned about losing money (they are typically older and wealthier).

Although it is hard to find direct research that points to folks with ASDs being more prone to Internet fraud than others, several of the characteristics listed previously suggest this would be the case. First, the amount of time a person is exposed to the Internet is a risk factor that makes individuals with high-functioning ASD vulnerable. Isolation, loneliness, and lack of perspective could make those with ASD much more prone to succumbing to such scams.

Lack of perspective may make it harder to recognize persuasive tactics with criminal motives. In addition, loneliness and isolation may make those with ASDs more likely to fall for Internet dating scams and to have fewer people with whom to talk and ask for advice during and after being scammed. This alone makes them more vulnerable. Finally, individuals with ASDs who also have ADHD issues, such as impulsivity, would be expected to take more risks, which is one of the characteristics associated with being a victim of fraud.

2

How to Prevent Cyber Bullying

Farrington and Ttofi studied the evidence for effective school-based programs to reduce bulling and victimization in general (ie, not specific only to cyber bullying).[7] The most effective programs shared the following key components: parent training and/or meetings, increased supervision in "hot spots" for bullying, implementation and management of classroom rules, development of a whole-school antibullying policy, enforcement of disciplinary methods, and longer duration and more intense training for children and teachers. In general, programs based on the work of Dan Olweus worked best. The Olweus antibullying program contains the following core components (adapted from Olweus, Limber, and Mihalic):[8]

I **Prerequisite Level**

There is an awareness of the problem of bullying, as well as the commitment and involvement of adults, such as school staff and parents. This is usually accomplished by distributing questionnaires to identify the extent of bullying behaviors going on in the school community.

II **School Level**

a. School surveys of bullying are conducted.

b. A school conference day is held for program administrators to review the results of the surveys and to discuss antibullying programs and how to implement them in school.

c. An antibullying committee is created to guide implementation efforts. The committee includes school staff, parents, and students.

d. There is increased supervision of "hot spots" for bullying, as identified in the survey (eg, the lunch room, the playground, and classrooms).

III **Class Level**

a. Class rules against bullying are created and enforced.

b. Regular class meetings are held to increase the understanding of bullying and its effects.

c. Meetings with parents are conducted to gain their involvement in reinforcing antibullying concepts.

IV Individual Level

a. The adults involved have serious talks with bullies (which may involve discipline) and victims (to help support and protect them from future bullying).

b. School personnel have serious talks with the parents of involved students.

The scope of the Olweus program points to the need to involve the entire school community—teachers, administrators, students, and parents—to effectively reduce bullying. Everyone needs to be sensitized to what constitutes bullying and the harm it causes and to support each other in reducing it. It is about changing the school culture to discourage bullying behavior.

Cyber bullying, even more so than other forms of bullying, often happens outside of school and is not immediately apparent to teachers and parents unless students report it. Thus, it is critical that students themselves adopt the attitude that it is wrong and are able to police themselves. To this end, students need to discourage each other from these behaviors and to report incidents to school staff or parents. This can be done confidentially, so they need not anticipate retaliation from accused bullies.

To reduce bullying and exclusion among students with ASDs, I have outlined sensitivity lessons for typically developing peers and information on how to create peer buddy programs, where students protect individuals with ASDs in the school environment (see Baker [9,10]). One of our programs to reduce bullying in a New Jersey middle school was highlighted by ABC World News in 2006.[11]

What should we teach children to reduce cyber bullying?

The following bullet points outline important issues to explain and teach to our children. To help them remember these points and live by them, we can give them two contracts to read and agree to: The "Be a Hero, Not a Bully" contract (Appendix A) and the "Use of Phone and Internet" contract (Appendix B).

I   **Teach children the definitions of what cyber bullying is:**

> Posting insulting and embarrassing information or pictures on a Web site

> Fooling victims into disclosing personal or sensitive information that bullies will later use against them

> Sending threatening or insulting messages directly to victims

> Impersonating others to send insulting or embarrassing messages

II   **Explain to them the risks and consequences of cyber bullying.**

> There is nothing anonymous online. Anything posted on the Internet or via cell phone can potentially be traced back to the creator. Words and pictures can be copied and forwarded and end up in the hands of school staff or angry parents of victims who may file complaints with the school or the police.

➤ Many schools are now required by state law to investigate accusations of cyber bullying, even when they do not involve school Web sites or when they occur after school hours. When instances of bullying are confirmed, the events will go on the perpetrators' school record, and there may be disciplinary actions, depending on the school's code of discipline.

➤ Victims of cyber bullying can file a police report, and there can be legal consequences for online bullying, including jail time for convicted perpetrators. It is crucial that students understand the potentially serious consequences of their texts and Internet posts.

➤ Explain the real-world effects of cyber bullying on its victims, including causing depression, anxiety, poor health, poor grades, and, in some tragic cases, suicide.

III Teach children that reducing bullying is everyone's responsibility: Be an upstander (someone who stands up for others), not just a bystander! My motto is, "Be a hero, not a bully!"

illustration by Justin Canha

➤ In most bullying situations, there are three roles: bully, victim, and bystander. Bystanders make up the largest and most influential group. They have a responsibility to protect others from being victimized and to stop their friends from bullying. It takes everyone (students, staff, and parents) to remind each other what kinds of texts, pictures, and information are not okay to communicate.

➤ It is best to try to stop others from bullying before it happens. If it does happen, reporting it is not the same as tattling. Tattling is when we report on events that are not dangerous and cause no harm. We do not have to tell on others for chewing gum in school, for example. However, when there is the potential to cause harm or create danger, as is the case with bullying, then reporting it is the brave thing to do and leads to greater safety for all.

➤ Reporting acts of bullying can be done anonymously in most schools. The reporter can ask that his or her name not be given to the alleged bully, to avoid any threat of retaliation.

IV **Teach your children not to be afraid to talk with you if they are aware of cyber bullying going on or if they are being bullied themselves. Explain that you will not take away their Internet privileges, as this fear often keeps kids from reporting cyber bullying.**

V **Parents can make rules for managing cell phone and Internet communications.**

➤ Make it clear that as long as parents pay for their children's Internet access and cell phones, as parents, they have a right to access those devices at any time. Even if they do not pay for these services, parents have a right to monitor their children's devices, since they are responsible for their children's behavior. Parents should have access to any passwords used for cell phones, e-mail accounts, and other messaging accounts. If children want to communicate entirely private messages to each other, they should do it face to face.

> Try to place Internet and cell phone devices in common areas, so parents can supervise all communications. This may not always be possible or practical, however, so children should turn in their devices to their parents before bedtime. This protects children from conducting hours of unsupervised communication and allows parents to periodically check on the nature of their child's communications.

> Never give out passwords, PIN numbers, or other information that allows others to pose as you on the Web or through e-mail. Similarly, do not let others use your phone to send texts from your number.

> Use "Netiquette"—be polite to others online, as any negative communication can be forwarded to others and can escalate into a conflict.

> Don't send messages when you are angry. You cannot take back what you have sent, so wait until you have calmed down before messaging.

> Don't open a message from someone you don't know, as it could be from a potential predator or bully.

What can you do if you are
a victim of cyber bullying?

(Adapted from *www.mysecurecyberspace.com/encyclopedia/index/cyberbullying.html*)[12]

➤ Don't reply to cyber bullying messages, other than telling the bully to stop. Bullies want you to get upset, so do not give them the pleasure of knowing that they got to you. It will only encourage them to do it more.

➤ Save threatening e-mails as evidence. Set your child's e-mail account to send all messages from a cyber bully to a specific folder.

➤ You can trace threatening e-mails or text messages. If your child receives threatening or harassing e-mails, forward them to "abuse@<domain name of provider>" (the domain name follows the "@" sign in the cyber bully's e-mail address) and request that the cyber bully's account be terminated. You can also use e-mail tracking software, such as eMailTrackerPro, which can trace the computer that an e-mail came from and automatically report harassing e-mails from the cyber bully's Internet Protocol (IP) address. If the harassment occurs via cell phone text messages, you can contact your phone company to trace the sender. If the threats are severe enough, contact your local police for help.

➤ Have offensive Web sites removed from the Internet. If threats or offensive comments about your child are being posted on a Web site, you can contact the hosting company to request that the site be taken down. You can find the host of the Web site by going to *Whois.net* and typing in the Web site address.

➤ Contact your child's school. Some schools are required by state law to investigate reported instances of cyber bullying. At the very least, the school may be able to provide counseling or mediation between your child and the accused cyber bully, if they attend the same school.

➤ Block the instant messaging (IM) accounts of cyber bullies. If cyber bullying is occurring over IM, you

can stop the harasser from contacting you. In many IM systems, you can block a user by clicking the "Block" button in the chat window.

➤ You may be able to sue a cyber bully or the bully's parents for damages if you can prove defamation, invasion of privacy, or intentional infliction of emotional distress. Damages can include money spent on counseling and limited college opportunities due to failing grades, for example.

➤ If cyber bullying becomes severe and involves threats of violence, you should contact the police immediately. Some states have computer harassment laws that allow prosecution of offenders.

➤ Victims of cyber bullying may benefit from counseling to protect their self-esteem and improve their coping skills. Counseling may involve:

    a. Understanding that victims of cyber bullying are not the ones with a problem. The people doing the bullying are the ones with problems.

    b. Discovering that they are not the only victims. Meeting in a group with other students who have been teased or bullied may be helpful in offsetting the isolation and self-doubts.

    c. Learning about famous and/or successful

people who were bullied as kids because of their looks or their learning and behavioral characteristics. This list includes President Obama (who was teased about his ears), Rihanna (who was teased about her skin color), Bill Gates, Einstein, Thomas Edison, and Temple Grandin, who were all teased for having social and learning differences. It seems the teasers were all wrong about these talented individuals. As Bill Gates once said, "Be kind to the nerds, because you are going to work for one later in life."

d. Learning to report the incidences of cyber bullying without shame. Victims of cyber bullying should not feel ashamed. They need to know that there are adults who will protect them, and reporting bullying is the brave thing to do. Parents and school officials must make sure that reports are taken seriously and not just dismissed as being typical kid behavior. It is often helpful for repeat victims to be asked weekly by their counselor if any teasing or bullying is going on or if any negative remarks are being made about them, as many victims will not report this type of behavior without being directly asked about it. Contrary to popular belief, asking about it will not make the child fabricate being a victim. So, check in regularly with those who have been victims!

3

How to Protect Kids from Online Predators

As with cyber bullying, the first line of defense is for parents to know with whom their kids are communicating and which devices they are using. Since the statistics demonstrate that teens are most likely to be victims, setting some ground rules with teens is important, even though it will be more challenging, given their desire for privacy and independence. Some of the same rules described for cyber bullying apply here, as well:

> ➤ Make it clear that as long as parents pay for their children's Internet and cell phones, they have a right as parents to access those devices at any time. Even if they are not paying for these services, parents have a right to monitor their children's Internet use, as they are responsible for their children's behavior. Parents should have access to any passwords

used for cell phones, e-mails, and other messaging accounts. If children want to communicate entirely private messages to each other, they should do it face to face.

➤ Try to place Internet and cell phone devices in common areas, so parents can supervise communications. This may not always be possible or practical, however, so children should turn in their devices to their parents before bedtime. This will protect children from conducting hours of unsupervised communication and allow parents to periodically check on the nature of their communications.

➤ Never give out passwords or PIN numbers to anyone, as they could access your private information and pose as you when communicating with others. Although kids often exchange other personal information with their friends, such as the names of other friends or family members, their address, phone number, and school name (or team name if you play sports), DO NOT SHARE THIS INFORMATION WITH STRANGERS. The statistics on victims of predators show that directly providing private information to strangers is associated with a greater risk of victimization. In addition, select strong passwords that are hard to guess. Use at least eight characters, including both letters and numbers. Avoid using common, recognizable words, and select a mix of lowercase and uppercase letters.

➤ Use "Netiquette"—be polite to others online. Using nasty language seems to attract online predators.

➤ Don't open a message from someone you don't know, as this could be from a potential predator.

➤ Don't believe everything you see or read. Predators often pose as different people. A 50-year-old male predator could easily steal pictures to pose as a 15-year-old girl looking to date 15-year-old boys.

➤ Explain to your children that it is always best to report any threats or scary messages to their parents. Predators often try to blackmail their victims by getting them to admit to rules they broke, then threatening to tell their parents this information unless the victim supplies pictures or agrees to meet with them. It is important to tell children that they will not get in trouble, as long as they tell their parents if any such threat is made.

> Teens should be warned about visiting online porn sites, as these are often predatory hot spots. Particularly, any site that shows underage people without clothes or engaged in sexual activity is both illegal and a haven for predators. Not only could a teen going on this site draw the attention of a predator, but he or she could also draw the attention of federal investigators who track child porn sites and those who visit or exchange pictures on them.

➤ You can track and filter communications from potential predators by using software like the following:

   a. eMailTrackerPro allows you to track Internet e-mails back to the IP address of the sender.

   b. McAfee Parental Controls software (and other antivirus software) offers chat-filtering protection for both IM and chat rooms.

   c. Predator Guard (from Security Soft) scans text on the computer screen, detects when that text could be threatening to the user's well-being, and ends the IM or chat session if the user chooses. The software can log "violations" or messages that contain language a sexual predator might use, to be used as evidence by law enforcement. The product contains a "library" of about 250 terms and phrases typically used by sexual predators and a system to detect and log that text to save as evidence.

➤ Set video game rules. Video games often allow Internet communication among players, making some players vulnerable to predators. You can set parental controls to limit Internet access, restrict games rated "mature," password-protect purchases, and set time limits on game use. (See *www.onguardonline.*

gov/articles/0270-kids-parents-and-video-games.[13])

a. Game-rating restrictions: This setting allows you to select which games can be played on the system or hand-held device on the basis of the rating from the Entertainment Software Rating Board. If you choose to allow your child to play games rated "teen" or older, you may want to limit Internet access.

b. Disabling or filtering Internet access: This setting can prevent your kids from accessing online features, such as online chatting. Some systems give parents the ability to approve friend requests or create approved lists of friends so they can continue to access the Internet with only certain people.

c. Time limits: Some game systems let you set days and times your kids can play and for how long.

d. In-game purchase restrictions: Sometimes, gaming systems allow you to buy downloadable games or content with the credit card that is tied to your account. In most cases, however, you can set a password to restrict those purchases.

4

Don't Be a Victim of Internet Scams

The best way to avoid becoming a victim is to familiarize yourself with the types of scams that are out there. I will review some of the currently popular Internet scams. First, however, there are some general rules you can follow to protect yourself from these scams.

General Rules to Protect Yourself from Scams

1. Do not give out personal account information, passwords, or your Social Security number to anyone you do not know. If someone calls or e-mails you to get that information by claiming they are from your bank or credit card company, do not give this information to them. Instead, contact your bank or credit card company through their official Web site or telephone number. Don't ever click on a link to a site provided through e-mail. Don't e-mail personal or financial information, as e-mail is not

a secure method of transmitting this kind of data. Only provide personal or financial information through an organization's Web site if you typed in the Web address yourself and you see signals that the site is secure, like a URL that begins with "https" (the "s" stands for "secure").

2. Do not wire or send cash to anyone. When you wire money, it cannot be retrieved easily. Making purchases with a credit card has some built-in protections, if you should later discover that the charges were fraudulent and you want to cancel the payment.

3. Use trusted security software and set it to update automatically to block spam and malware from downloading to your computer.

4. Review credit card and bank account statements as soon as you receive them to check for unauthorized charges. If your statement is late, call to confirm your billing address and account balances, as someone may have made changes to your account if they stole your identity.

5. Do not open attachments, click on links, or download files from e-mails, unless a known person said they were going to send them to you ahead of time.

These files can contain viruses or other malware that can weaken your computer's security. They may have been sent automatically from a friend or a colleague's computer that had a virus. Always check with your friend to see if he or she intended to send you the file before opening it.

6. THE MOST IMPORTANT RULE: Ask someone you do trust (like a parent or trusted counselor) before agreeing to any new contract or giving information to anyone you do not know.

Common Online Scams

(Adapted from *www.onguardonline.gov/topics/avoid-scams*)[14]

Work-at-Home Scams

The Bait:

Ads promise a high income for home-based work, often in medical claims processing, online searching, international shipping, rebate processing, envelope stuffing, data entry, shopping, setting up an e-commerce site, or assembling crafts. Example ads say things like:

➤ "Be part of one of America's fastest growing industries."

- ➤ "Be your own boss."
- ➤ "Earn thousands of dollars every month from your own home."
- ➤ "Call our 1-900 number."
- ➤ "Get paid to shop!"

The Catch:

The ads don't say you may have to spend your own money first to begin the job. You may never get the salary you were promised after you pay them the money to begin the job. For example, one kind of work-at-home scam is the "e-commerce plan." An e-commerce scammer will claim that after you pay a one-time setup fee for an e-commerce site, all you have to do is encourage people to go to a certain Web site to make purchases. If you use your online presence to encourage others to shop on this site, the scammer claims you will get a small amount of money from each sale. So you pay the scammer money, and you may never get paid in return.

Lotteries and Sweepstakes Scams

The Bait:

You get a letter or an e-mail message that claims you've already won a foreign lottery or an online sweepstakes. The letter may appear to be from a government agency, a bank, or some other company. The letter indicates that to claim your winnings, you need to write a check or wire money to cover taxes, fees, shipping costs, or insurance.

Examples of fake lotteries and/or subject lines include "European Union International Lottery International Winners/Prize Awards," "The Desk of the Global Share Promotional Notification: Amsterdam, The Netherlands," "Government Accredited Licensed Lottery Promoters: Winning Notice for Category B Winner," "Microsoft Mega Jackpot Lottery Promotions," and "Swiss Lotto Zurich High Stakes International Promotions Lottery."

The Catch:

Once you transfer the money, you cannot get it back, and there are no actual lottery winnings.

Fake Check Scams

The Bait:

You get an actual check in the mail for "part of your lottery winnings" and are asked to wire money (less than the amount in the check sent to you) to cover the cost of sending you "the rest of the winnings." So it appears you would come out ahead, even if you

wire the money requested. An alternative scam is that you receive a large check in the mail as an overpayment for a response to your ad or online auction posting. The buyer asks that you wire back the amount overpaid for the item after you deposit the check.

The Catch:

The check looks real, and the bank will accept it. But, days later, you will discover that the check bounced. If you have already wired money, you cannot get it back.

Imposter Scams

The Bait:

You get a call, e-mail, or text from someone claiming to be a family member or friend who says he needs you to wire cash to help him out of a terrible situation, because someone has stolen his money or he has been in a terrible accident. He may say he needs the money to fix a car, get out of jail, pay a hospital bill, or leave a foreign country. But, he wants you to keep his request a secret from others. There might be a second person in this scheme—someone who claims to be an authority figure, like a judge, lawyer, or police officer. These callers may claim that your friend won't be allowed to leave the country unless you send money right away.

The Catch:

These people are in fact strangers who are just trying to steal your money.

Bogus Apartment Rentals

The Bait:

In your search for an apartment or vacation rental, you find a great property at an incredible price. They say you can have the property if you wire money for an application fee, security deposit, or the first month's rent. The owners might say they're out of the country, but they have someone who can get you the keys.

The Catch:

There is no actual property; they are just stealing your money. Only agree to rent from known rental companies or from landlords you know through others who have rented.

Debt Relief Scams

The Bait:

A company promises to consolidate your bills into one monthly payment, without having to borrow more. They

claim this will stop you from being harassed by credit card companies, prevent you from undergoing foreclosure or repossession, help you avoid tax levies and garnishments, and wipe out your debts.

The Catch:

These offers often require you to declare bankruptcy, which has a long-term negative effect on your credit scores, can stay on your credit report for up to 10 years, and can hurt your ability to get credit, a job, insurance, or even a place to live. You may also have to pay fees to an attorney to be able to file for bankruptcy. Get more accurate information about debt relief and bankruptcy from the Federal Trade Commission (FTC) before embarking on this serious step.

Pay-in-Advance Credit Offers

The Bait:

You get the great news that you've been "prequalified" to get a low-interest loan or credit card and/or to be able to repair your bad credit. To activate the loan or credit repair, you have to send a processing fee of several hundred dollars.

The Catch:

There is no loan coming.

Investment Schemes

The Bait:

Offers promise investments that have high rates of return, with little or no risk. A company or a representative may explain that they have insider information and can guarantee the investment, or they'll buy it back. They may show phony, complicated statistics that play on your desire to act like you know what they are talking about. They usually want you to act quickly, or the opportunity will no longer be available.

The Catch:

If an investment seems too good to be true, it probably is. Take your time before acting on any investment decision. Obtaining and acting upon insider information is illegal, so that should be a red flag not to invest. Ask for advice from trusted advisors, counselors, or attorneys before investing. Many of these schemes do not have a long history, as predators take the investor's money and then close down quickly. So, check to see if the investment has a long public track record. If not, it could be a scam.

The "Nigerian" E-mail Scam

The Bait:

The people behind these messages claim to be officials, businesspeople, or the surviving spouses of former government honchos in Nigeria or another country, whose money is tied up temporarily. They offer to transfer lots of money into your bank account if you will pay the fees or "taxes" they need to get their money. If you respond to the initial offer, you may receive documents that look "official." They may even encourage you to travel to the country in question, or a neighboring country, to complete the transaction. Some fraudsters have produced trunks of phony dyed or stamped money to try to verify their claims. Although e-mail scams may originate from other countries, currently, 51% of all e-mail scams come from Nigeria. So if you see the word "Nigeria" in an unknown e-mail, you can assume it is a scam.

The Catch:

The e-mails are from crooks who are trying to steal your money or your identity. Inevitably, "emergencies" will come up, requiring you to spend more of your money and delaying the "transfer of funds" to your account. In the end, there aren't any profits for you and your money is gone, along with the thief who stole it. According to State Department reports, people who have responded to these e-mails have been beaten, subjected to threats and extortion, and, in some cases, murdered.

Online Dating Scams

The Bait:

A prospective romantic partner befriends you over the Internet. He or she slowly hooks you in, claiming his love and attraction for you. Eventually he needs money for some emergency to cover:

> - Travel expenses
> - Medical emergencies
> - Hotel bills
> - Hospital bills for a child or other relative
> - Visas or other official documents
> - Losses from a temporary financial setback, a mugging, or a robbery

The Catch:

The person was only pretending to be interested in you to eventually get your money. Do not wire any money to cover this person's expenses. Report relationship scams to the FTC, the Federal Bureau of Investigation's (FBI's) Internet Crime Complaint Center, or your state attorney general.

Tech Support Scams, "Phishing" Scams, and Identity Theft

The Bait:

You get an e-mail or phone call, telling you there has been some kind of security problem with one of your accounts or your computer system.

Common messages read as follows:

➤ "We suspect there has been an unauthorized transaction on your account. To ensure that your account is not compromised, please click the link below and confirm your identity."

➤ "During our regular verification of accounts, we couldn't verify your information. Please click here to update and verify your information."

➤ "Our records indicate that your account was over-charged. You must call us within 7 days to receive your refund."

➤ "Your computer has been exposed to a virus or malware. To fix it, we will need to verify your account information."

The Catch:

The senders of these messages are "phishing" for your personal information, so they can use it to steal your identity and commit fraud. They may be trying to install malware software on your computer when you click on their links so they can steal your personal information. They are not offering any real service.

"Phishing" means trying to get personal information from you to be able to steal your identity or commit fraud. If you receive messages that you suspect are part of a "phishing" scam, delete the e-mails and text messages that ask you for personal information (credit card and bank account numbers, Social Security numbers, passwords, PIN numbers, etc). Legitimate companies don't ask for this information via e-mail or text. The predators might threaten to "close your account" or take other action if you don't respond. Don't reply, and don't click on links or call phone numbers provided in the message. One trick that can help you determine if an e-mail is a phishing scam is to move your cursor over the link the e-mail asks you to click on. Let your cursor hover there, but don't click on the link! A Web address will appear under your cursor, which may or may not match the Web address where the link is supposed to go. If the Web address that appears under your cursor does NOT match the Web address shown, or if it is mostly a numeric URL with few or no words or letters, then the

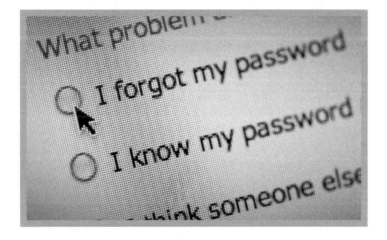

e-mail is a phishing scam. If you're concerned about your account or you want to reach an actual organization you do business with, call the number on your financial statements or on the back of your credit card.

It is a good idea to report "phishing" e-mails. Forward these e-mails to *spam@uce.gov* and to the company, bank, or organization impersonated in the e-mail. You may also report phishing e-mails to *reportphishing@antiphishing.org*. Or, you can forward them to "abuse@<your e-mail provider>" (eg, *abuse@aol.com*).

What if your personal information is lost or stolen or you believe you are a victim of identity theft?

Put a Fraud Alert on Your Credit Reports

Contact one of these three nationwide credit-reporting companies and ask them to put a fraud alert on your credit report:

Equifax: (800) 525-6285
Experian: (888) 397-3742
TransUnion: (800) 680-7289

Any one company you call must contact the others. They will place a fraud alert on your file, which will make it harder for an identity thief to open any accounts in your

name. The alert stays in effect for 90 days. If you create an Identity Theft Report (see the following), you can ask for an extended alert on your file beyond 90 days.

Review Your Credit Reports

After you place a fraud alert on your file, you are allowed to receive one free copy of your credit report from each credit reporting company. Check the reports to see if your personal information is correct and if there are any accounts you did not open or debts that are not yours. If there are accounts or debts you did not create, contact the credit-reporting companies to report the fraud and have them corrected. You may also want to contact the fraud department at any company where an account was opened without your permission. Ask the company to send you proof that they corrected or closed the problem accounts.

Create an Identity Theft Report

An Identity Theft Report will help you get fraudulent information removed permanently from your credit report, prevent companies from collecting debts that result from identity theft or selling the debts to others for collection, and put an extended fraud alert on your credit report.

To create an Identity Theft Report:

1. File an identity theft complaint with the FTC online at *http://ftc.gov/idtheft* or by phone at (877) 438-4338.

2. When you file with the FTC, make sure to get a copy of the FTC affidavit that shows the details of your complaint. The online complaint site explains how to print your completed affidavit. If you file your complaint by phone, ask the counselor how to get a copy of your affidavit.

3. Take your completed FTC identity theft affidavit and go to your local police, or the police at the location where the theft occurred, to file a police report. Get a copy of the police report or the report number.

The FTC identity theft affidavit plus a police report makes an Identity Theft Report. Send copies of the Identity Theft Report to the companies where you reported accounts you never opened or purchases you never made. Ask them to remove or correct fraudulent information in your accounts.

5

An Insider's View of Keeping Safe in the Digital World

by Jennifer McIlwee Myers

Hello. My name is Jennifer, and I have Asperger's syndrome. As someone who does not want to fall prey to scams, hoaxes, or rip-offs online, I have had to develop skills and habits to keep me safe. (So far, so good!) Jed Baker is kindly allowing me to contribute a few hints and tips from my own experiences, including a list of Web sites that help me use the Internet safely.

Web Sites I Recommend Visiting Regularly

No one can know every possible variation of online scams and hoaxes, and there are far too many major variations to list them all in this book. Because of this, I regularly spend time going over recent examples. It is hard for those of us on the autism spectrum to generalize well enough to be able to recognize new variations on old scams, but by looking at many specific examples, I can force my brain to mimic generalization.

The sources listed here are full of information and examples that demonstrate exactly what hoaxes, Internet scams, and predatory e-mails and Web sites look like.

These resources have helped me greatly and can be read and discussed with your spouse, your children, and/or other people in your life who are on the spectrum.

snopes.com

Snopes.com is a venerable source of information, clarifications, and debunking for every sort of Internet rumor, scam, and urban legend. Spend some time looking at the most recent hoaxes. There is a link on the home page called, "What's New." This will take you to a list of the most recent Internet hoaxes and scams.

It is important to note that *snopes.com* addresses many kinds of rumors and hoaxes, not just those that are immediately dangerous or involve directly harming or scamming people. This is important because when a child or teen forwards an e-mail or posts something to Facebook about an urban legend or a hoax as if it were true, it calls attention to their naïveté. Facebook is a very public place, and e-mails that are forwarded get forwarded again and again. If your child has forwarded hoaxes or posted them online, then bullies or scammers may single him out as a target on that basis alone.

The more you know what urban legends and scams look like, the harder you are to fool, and the less foolish you look on the Internet.

hoax-slayer.com

Hoax Slayer is a very large and detailed Web site that offers information about hundreds of scams, with examples. This site has an easy-to-use search function. Habitually search-ing for the subject of any "odd" or suspicious e-mail or online information on this site will keep you from falling into many traps.

consumerist.com

The Consumerist is a blog about all kinds of consumer problems, including e-mail and Internet scams, as well as how to deal with being ripped off online. Again, this site deals with many different kinds of situations, not just e-mail or online dangers.

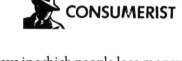

The short posts about the ways in which people lose money to unscrupulous online and off-line scammers are generally readable and often entertaining.

consumerreports.org and *Consumer Reports* magazine

These two resources are not free, but they can usually be
found through your local library. *Consumer Reports* maga-
zine frequently has articles about topics like electronics
and privacy and features reviews about computer security
software on a regular basis.

Consumer Reports is **ConsumerReports**®
usually available at public
libraries, and I highly recommend that you consult recent
issues to see what computer security suites it features.
Reviews of free or low-cost software are usually included,
making it fairly easy to find software that can keep you or
your child safe on a budget.

Four Internet Safety Concepts That Have Helped Me

The Internet is almost like a foreign country, with its own culture and mores. Some ideas that are often talked about are:

    I. Using strong passwords
   II. Godwin's Law
 III. Rule 34
 IV. The Streisand Effect

Understanding these four things has helped me keep safe, prevent useless arguments, avoid Web sites I don't want to visit, and not make a laughingstock of myself online.

Whether you want to share these with your child will depend on his age, maturity, and level of understanding, but the first concept is so important that I hope you will talk with your child about it repeatedly over the years. Some things are worth talking about again and again.

I | **Using Strong Passwords**

Creating a strong password is discussed often by Internet security experts. Weak passwords can easily and quickly compromise your safety online.

In most cases, the first, last, and only defense you and your child will have against having his Facebook or other accounts cracked is his password. It is quick and easy for a bully or crook to run a script (a small computer program) to try every single possible word in the English language and every likely combination of words, and it takes little more time to check against dictionaries of the major spoken languages of the world.

Because of this, computer security experts strongly urge the development of what are called "strong" passwords, which are passwords that are hard to guess, even with the help of scripts. A strong password meets the following criteria. It contains:

➤ Both letters and numbers
➤ Both lowercase and uppercase letters
➤ At least eight characters
➤ No recognizable words
➤ No texting-type abbreviations

Also, you should never use the same password for different accounts or Web sites.

Understanding what makes a password strong has helped me avoid having my passwords guessed or "cracked." Please discuss the importance of password selection with your child!

II **Godwin's Law**

Godwin's Law is a watchword of Internet discussion groups. It was first stated in 1990 by Mike Godwin, and it simply says that the longer any Internet argument goes on, the more likely it is that one side or the other will start comparing their opponents to Hitler or Nazis.

How on earth could something like this help a person stay safe on the Internet? Well, it's generally understood by persons who have good "Netiquette" that once Godwin's Law is in action—once a discussion or argument starts, involving calling people bad names and associating them with horrible historic figures— that argument is effectively over, and no one will really have anything good to say.

Once a discussion online devolves into name-calling or personal attacks, it is best to simply walk away from the discussion. As an Aspie, I tend to want to win all arguments. Being wrong is not something

I like even a tiny bit, and I can keep arguing longer than anyone.

But, Godwin's Law tells us that eventually, no one "wins" the original argument because all of the participants get farther and farther from discussing anything of any importance as the argument continues.

Having developed a basic understanding of Godwin's Law, you have no idea how much it has saved me from experiencing unnecessary stress, anguish, and wasted time. While young children and some teens will not understand how Godwin's Law pertains to Internet discussions, it is likely to be a great help if parents and teachers are aware of this law and can discuss with their children what it says about the nature of arguing on the Internet.

III **Rule 34**

Rule 34 is not the 34th of any set of rules anyone knows. It is a rule that was made up as a joke, as part of a cartoon, that became well known throughout the Internet because it is so very true. Rule 34 states that "If it exists, someone has made porn out of it. No exceptions." Well, good heavens. How on earth could knowing this make me feel safer online?

Quite simply, knowing what is out there helps me avoid it. When people are naive about the nature of what can be found online, they are less likely to be able to protect themselves and others from unwanted information, visuals, and general creepiness.

I'm not afraid of pictures of naked people, and I'm pretty sure stumbling onto old copies of *Playboy* will not cause actual harm to humans. Nonetheless, I do not want to stumble onto the fan art of someone who thinks of Rainbow Brite and He-Man very differently than I do. That stuff can burn itself into your brain on sight. As they say, "You can't un-see things."

Would I explain Rule 34 to a child? No. Would I explain it to a teen on the autism spectrum? Maybe, depending on what he or she asks about. But, it's not about your child or teen knowing Rule 34. It's about parents, guardians, and teachers being aware of what's out there. Setting restrictions on your child's Internet search engines can prevent innocent eyes from seeing their favorite Disney characters in disturbing sexual positions.

If your children do pull up inappropriate content, they need to know they won't be punished for one or two wrong clicks. If your children are afraid that finding something inappropriate will get them into trouble, they will do their best to hide it, if they do find such content. If that happens, they won't be able to talk to you about it, and that means missing the chance for you to be able to deal with it properly.

No software in the world can keep your child safe from problematic sites all the time. A program can screen sites for key-words and key phrases, which is often helpful and never sufficient. Such "nanny" software can provide some help, but it isn't enough. You have to be there and be aware. You have to  remember that there is no substitute in the world for a parent who has open eyes and ears and an open heart.

Rule 34 means there is no perfect filter and that someone young who doesn't expect troublesome sites to pop up is vulnerable to some problematic stuff. Make sure your child can rely on you to monitor his activities when he is online.

IV The Streisand Effect

Last but not least, let's talk about the Streisand Effect. This is a well-known Internet phenomenon that can happen on a large or a very small scale. Understanding it taught me that sometimes, it is best to leave well enough alone.

Here is a brief history of this phenomenon. In 2003, Barbara Streisand got upset. A set of aerial photos taken to show the erosion of the California coast was available online, and one of them showed her house. She sued the photographer for invasion of privacy. Before she sued, no one had noticed that among the set of 12,000 photos, Streisand's home could be seen in one photo. In fact, only six people had downloaded the image! Then the lawsuit hit the news, and hundreds of thousands of people flocked to see the image that created all the fuss.

The lesson? Shouting loudly (either literally or figuratively) about something you don't want anyone to see is not a good thing to do on the Internet.

I cannot tell you how many times I have seen people send huge amounts of traffic to other people's Facebook pages by posting about how awful and terrible another person (or their Facebook page) is. It is hard (very hard) to see things posted about yourself online or to get nasty e-mails and text messages and to NOT reply loudly and clearly. Again, as an Aspie, my gut instinct is always to go into full-on argument mode the second anyone says anything against me or sends me an insulting e-mail.

But, the Streisand effect works on the small scale of middle-school fights and similar adult tiffs. If you get an insulting text message and reply vehemently, you have now provided your attacker with something he or she can send to anyone and everyone. If you had simply saved the insulting message and, if necessary, told the appropriate authorities, you could have avoided getting yourself into a heap of trouble.

Having public tantrums and meltdowns is one of the hardest things to overcome when you're on the autism spectrum. In the end, such meltdowns just draw more negative attention to you. It may seem like a great idea to tell the world about what a horrible bully that nasty girl in your 3rd period reading class is, but once you've e-mailed or posted about it, anyone can save your words and share them. At this point, if you were the one who decided to "out" the mean girl, bully, or jerk, then you will be the one who is deemed a bully, and you could possibly get into serious trouble. Heed Jed Baker's advice: "Don't send messages when you are angry. You cannot take back what you have sent, so wait until you have calmed down before messaging" (found on page 23 of this book).

What Barbara Streisand inadvertently taught us is that going on the warpath can have serious consequences. Knowing this has helped me remember to keep quiet about personal conflicts online or at least to be very, very careful in that area. It's an important concept in the online culture, and it can help you keep your child safe.

A

APPENDIX:
"Be a Hero, Not a Bully" Contract

I **What is cyber bullying?**

a. Cyber bullying means posting insulting and/or embarrassing information or pictures on a Web site or through some other form of online media. Remember, what may not be embarrassing to you may be to others, so don't post anything about others without their permission.

Examples include making negative comments about someone else's pictures, videos, characteristics, race, religion, appearance, or behaviors, such as, "She looks ugly," "His voice is terrible," or "He is so gay."

b. Getting people to tell you personal information that you may later use to embarrass them is also a form of cyber bullying.

An example would be posting information online about someone your friend has a crush on.

c. It can mean sending threatening or insulting messages directly to others.

Examples might include threatening to beat someone up, telling a lie about them, and insulting their looks, race, sexual orientation, behavior, or other characteristics.

d. Cyber bullying also can mean impersonating others to send insulting or embarrassing messages.

Examples might include using someone else's password to log into their phone or online account and then sending texts or making comments as if you were him or her. Or, it could involve setting up an account in someone else's name or with some else's picture(s) so you can pose as that person. Their account and identify are then used to post embarrassing or insulting information.

II What are the consequences of cyber bullying?

a. With cyber bullying, you can get caught really easily. Anything you post on the Internet or through your cell phone can be traced back to you. Words and pictures can be copied and forwarded and end up in the hands of school staff or angry parents, who may file complaints against you!

b. Many schools are required to investigate accusations of cyber bullying among their students, even when they do not involve school Web sites or when they occur after school hours. If it is confirmed that you cyber bullied someone, it can go on your permanent school record, and there may be disciplinary actions, like detentions, suspensions, expulsions, and possible involvement with the police.

c. Victims of cyber bullying can file a police report, which can result in legal consequences for online bullies. Some older students have received jail time for acts of cyber bullying.

d. Research shows that bullying can cause its victims to experience depression, anxiety, poor health, poor grades, and, in some tragic cases, suicide. Don't hurt others just because you think something is funny!

III **It is everyone's responsibility to stop bullying. Be an** *upstander* **(someone who stands up for others), not a bystander. "Be a hero, not a bully!"**

a. In most bullying situations, there are three roles: the bully (the one who hurts others), the victim (the one who gets hurt), and bystanders (those who see what is happening). Bystanders are the most powerful group, because they have the ability to be heroic and stop the bullying. They can tell others to stop or go to an adult for help.

b. As a general rule, try to stop others from bullying

before it happens. If it does happen, report it to an adult. This is not the same as tattling. Tattling is when we report events that are not dangerous and cause no harm. We do not have to tell on others for chewing gum in school, for example. However, when there is the potential to cause harm or create danger, as is the case with bullying, then reporting it is the brave thing to do and leads to greater safety for all.

c. Reporting acts of bullying can be done anonymously in most schools. The reporter can ask that his or her name not be given to the bully, to avoid any threat of retaliation.

IV **Don't be afraid to talk with your parents if you hear about or see cyber bullying going on or if you are being bullied yourself. You will not be punished or lose Internet or phone privileges for reporting these problems.**

I, _____,
understand what cyber bullying is and what the consequences of cyber bullying are. I agree not to cyber bully others, and, to the best of my ability, I will try to stop others or report others who engage in cyber bullying. In short, I will try to be a hero, not a bully.

_____   Date: _____

(signature of student)

_____   Date: _____

(signature of parent)

illustration by Justin Canha

APPENDIX:
Use of Phone and
Internet Contract

1. I understand that my parents bought and pay for my phone and Internet access. I am borrowing usage of these privileges from them. Even if they do not pay for these services, my parents are responsible for me and my behavior, since I am a minor. As such, they are entitled to know that I use these privileges safely and responsibly.

2. I will share the passwords for my phone and Internet accounts with my parents.

3. I will let my parents follow me on Facebook, Instagram, and other online accounts.

4. I will turn my phone in to my parents each weeknight evening at _____ PM and each weekend night at _____ PM. My phone will be turned off and returned to me in the morning.

5. I will NOT use the phone or Internet to engage in cyber bullying. This means I will not use profanity, make insulting or embarrassing remarks, lie, attempt to fool others, or impersonate anyone on the phone or Internet.

6. I will not send or receive nude pictures of myself, my private parts, or anyone else's, nor will I use the phone or Internet to access pornographic material. Some porn sites are illegal, particularly if they involve pictures of underage individuals. Sending or receiving nude pictures

of underage individuals can result in investigations by the police and/or the FBI.

7. If I lose my phone, I will tell my parents immediately, so we can stop strangers from using the phone. If I break the phone, I will contribute money to pay for replacement costs or repairs.

8. I will answer phone calls or texts from my parents. I will also put my phone down or away when others are talking to me directly, when we are socializing at a meal, or when I am talking with family members.

I, _____,
agree to the rules in this contract. I am not perfect and may break these rules sometimes, at which point my parents will take away my phone and/or Internet privileges for a period of time and discuss the problem with me. We will then start the contract over, and I will do my best to be more responsible in how I use the phone and Internet.

_____ Date: _____
(signature of student)

_____ Date: _____
(signature of parent)

1   Cyber Bullying Research Center. Summary of our cyberbullying research from 2004-2010. *www.cyberbullying.us/research.php*. Accessed May 15, 2013.

2   Sofronoff K, Dark E, Stone V. Social vulnerability and bullying in children with Asperger syndrome. *Autism*. 2011;15(3):355-372.

3   Kowalkski R, Fedina C. Cyber bullying in ADHD and Asperger syndrome populations. *Res Autism Spectrum Disord*. 2011;5:1201-1208.

4   Wolak J, Finkelhor D, Mitchell K, Ybarra M. Online "predators" and their victims: myths, realities, and implications for prevention and treatment. *Am Psychol*. 2008;63(2):111-128.

5   Titus RM, Gover AR. Personal fraud: the victims and the scams. National Institute of Justice, Washington, DC. *Crime Prev Stud*. 2008;12:133-151.

6   Pak K, Shadel D. AARP national fraud victim study. *Research and Strategic Analysis*, Washington DC. 2011. *http://assets.aarp.org/rgcenter/econ/fraud-victims-11.pdf*. Accessed May 20, 2013.

7   Farrington DP, Ttofi MM. School-based programs to reduce bullying and victimization. Systematic review for The Campbell Collaboration Crime and Justice Group; 2010. *www.ncjrs.gov/pdffiles1/nij/grants/229377.pdf*. Accessed May 15, 2013.

8   Olweus D, Limber SP, Mihalic S. *The Bullying Prevention Program: Blueprints for Violence Prevention*. Vol 10. Boulder, CO: Center for the Study and Prevention of Violence; 1999.

9   Baker JE. *Social Skills Training for Children and Adolescents with Aspergers Syndrome and Related Social Communication Disorders*. Shawnee Mission, KS: AAPC Publishing; 2003.

10 Baker JE. *Preparing for Life: The Complete Guide to Transitioning to Adulthood for Those with Autism and Asperger's Syndrome*. Arlington, TX: Future Horizons; 2005.

11 Echoes of autism [transcript]. *ABC World News*. ABC television. April 7, 2006.

12 My Secure Cyberspace. Cyberbullying. *www.mysecurecyberspace.com/encyclopedia/index/cyberbullying.html*. Accessed May 15, 2013.

13 On Guard Online. Kids, parents, and video games. *www.onguardonline.gov/articles/0270-kids-parents-and-video-games*. Accessed May 15, 2013.

14 On Guard Online. Avoid scams. *www.onguardonline.gov/topics/avoid-scams*. Accessed May 15, 2013.

Jed Baker, PhD, is the director of the Social Skills Training Project, an organization that serves individuals with autism and social communication problems. He is on the professional advisory board of *Autism Today*, the Asperger Autism Spectrum Education Network (ASPEN), Asperger's Network Support for Wellbeing, Education, and Research (ANSWER), the YAI Autism Center, the Kelberman Center, and several other autism organizations. In addition, he writes, lectures, and provides training internationally on the topic of social skills training and managing challenging behaviors. He is an award-winning author of five books, including *Social Skills Training for Children and Adolescents with Asperger Syndrome and Social-Communication Problems*; *Preparing for Life: The Complete Handbook for the Transition to Adulthood for Those with Autism and Asperger's Syndrome*; *The Social Skills Picture Book*; *The Social Skills Picture Book for High School and Beyond*; and *No More Meltdowns: Positive Strategies for Managing and Preventing Out-of-Control Behavior*. His work has also been featured on *ABC World News*, *Nightline*, *Fox News*, the *CBS Early Show*, and the Discovery Health Channel. Visit his Web site at *www.jedbaker.com* for more information.